When You Seek Me

When You Seek Me

Poems

by

Sister Paula Marie Beiter S.C.C.

To Martha —
Good reading.
May you enjoy
and be
enriched by
the poems.
Bless you.
Sister Paula Marie

Holy Spirit Creations
19 Old Depot Road
New Cumberland, PA 17070

Sr. Paula Marie Beiter, S.C.C.

ISBN Number: 0-9679004-0-9
Library of Congress Control Number
00-132373

Holy Spirit Creations, Publisher
19 Old Depot Road
New Cumberland, PA 17070-2439

Additional Copies available from the
Publisher by mail or E-mail.
Holyspiritcreations@dellnet.com

Printed in the United States of America
by Bookmasters, Inc., Mansfield, Ohio

Chapter introductions by William A. Fetterhoff

Cover photographs by Sister Nicholas Campasano, S.C.C.

Proceeds from sales to
Sisters of Christian Charity

I know the plans I have in mind for you.
When you seek me you shall find me,
When you seek me with all your heart;
I will let you find me.

Jeremiah 29: 11-14
Jerusalem Bible

Dedication

To Father Edward Salmon, S.J.
who encouraged me
to listen to the yearnings
of my heart.

CONTENTS

Chapter I   Searching

Chapter 2   Love and Commitment

Chapter 3 *Nature*

ACKNOWLEDGMENTS

My deepest gratitude to William Fetterhoff to whom I taught English many years ago in Reading, Pennsylvania. A lawyer now who I hope will one day write "the great American novel," Bill has been a constant and consistent support in the preparation and publication of this book. He it was who first suggested many years ago that the poems be published, and it was he who went through several hundred of my poems and selected those for inclusion in this book. He arranged them in the order in which you find them in this volume and wrote the chapter pages. "These should be read as a whole," he has said more than once. Bill has been my primary mentor in this undertaking, ever unflagging in his support and encouragement. Marilyn, his wife, has also been quietly affirming.

Reverend Edward Salmon, S.J., several years ago during retreat, urged me to pay attention to the yearnings of my heart. One of those yearnings was to return to writing poetry, a practice I had submerged in my busy-ness. Father Ed freed me to create again and during that retreat I wrote five or six poems that made me very happy. Over the years, he has been a very special grace in my life, my prayer life as well as my creative life. He has brought me closer to the Lord and to my creative self. He is strongly, quietly, and unseen, a great support and a dear friend.

Colonel David Farr came into my life several years ago. After his wife died, he joined my Bereavement Group and has become my second in command in arranging meetings and retreats. Since he learned of my book, he has sought out printers, executed the cover design, offered to underwrite the project, and done countless things to assure the success of the publication. He, too, is a blessing in my life. Without his support and encouragement, I doubtless would not have persevered in this undertaking.

Sister Rose William, a dear and true friend since we entered the convent together, has graciously typed my original copy and made corrections on my final copy. She is a careful reader and proofreader whose advice I value tremendously. I am grateful for all the time she has given so willingly to this project.

Sister Mary Andrea has offered valuable assistance in the technical aspects of the book. She has been wonderfully generous with her time and expertise.

Sister Mary Edward, SCC, my provincial, gave her unequivocal and enthusiastic support to this enterprise, as did Sister Mary Dorothy, my superior. Both have been rooting for me and are standing on the sidelines cheering.

Finally, I am grateful to all my dear Sisters at Holy Spirit whose love and interest have spurred me on. They are truly Sisters of Christian Charity whom I love deeply and dearly.

There are many others who have had a hand in this book, notably Sister Nicholas, whose photographs grace both the front and back covers; Sister Maria Weiman who prepared sketches for the poems only to learn that art work could be cost prohibitive; Jacquie Roland, an artist I met in Kingston, New York, who made sketches for me; and all the other wonderful people who had a part in making these pages a reality.

Most of all, I am grateful to the Lord who led me through darkness into light and gifted me with the ability to express in words and images the wonder of his life.

INTRODUCTION

Some years ago, I went through a deeply anguished period during which the Lord seemed hidden, dark, almost nonexistent. I went in search of him within and without, finding Him in neither place but paradoxically, knowing Him to be in both places.

Those months were painful ones in which I wandered sometimes aimlessly, sometimes out of control, but always united with the God unseen and unfelt except in deepest, darkest faith. In the Searching poems, this journey found a voice as I was able to pour out in poetry the thoughts of my heart.

Chapter 2, Love and Commitment, is a bursting forth of the seeking love in the quiet realization and deep certitude of the Lord's showering and caressing love. There is a surrender to the ineffable love of Him who lavished me with that love, walked unseen by my side, and enabled me to butterfly the spring with the freshness of His love and mine. Freed of the intense anguish of the darkness and the search, I could wonder at the Omnipotence that accommodated itself to me, to us.

From the resolution of the search, I looked to Nature from its smallest evocation to the cosmic glory of the radiant moon, from ancient trees deprived of limb to glorious snow feather frosted evergreens, and even to a mysterious intruder creating a gaping hole in a delicate spider's web.

It is my deepest hope that these poems will inspire the reader and that the experiences expressed will strike in each one a resonant note. I pray that the reader will come to the profound and beautiful realization that the Lord promises to let Himself be found if we but seek.

Chapter One

Searching

Yet was I sore afraid
Lest having Thee,
I should have none beside.
-Francis Thompson

O God! Thou has made us for thyself
and our souls are restless,
searching
till they find their rest in thee.
-St. Augustine

Through loneliness, disorientation
and chaos toward a glimmer of light, the
frustration and pain of anticipation; and then
a long day and night of the soul, through
stages toward nothingness, and at last,
through utter negation, to a perception of
transcendent love.

Bereft

Loneliness left me gasping
Flung onto the wet sandy beach
By a sudden spray of ocean
Unexpectedly violent

Lost

Fog shrouded the distant hills in a veil of
gauze
You were lost to view behind a bleak grey
mist
Wet brown stalks clawed my clothes
As I struggled through the dense underbrush
In search of you

You, Distant Light, Beckon

I cannot find my way in this chaos primeval
Where paths are chance and roads nonexist
No map guides my steps
No guide maps my way
I step hesitantly
Into this labyrinth of light and darkness
Only occasional glimpses through the thickets
To the clearing's distant light
Make the journey bearable

Where Are You?

I touch the back burner
To test its heat before putting the coffee on
My finger numbs to the pain dumbly
And I deposit the Pyrex pot
In its accustomed place
On the left rear burner
Even the delicious coffee savored
With family and friends
Fails to dispel the lost numb pain I feel
Without you

A Palpable Presence

I hear your voice in the ticking of the clock
The silent snow speaks eloquently of you
And the gentle rain weeps with me
Overflowing in tearful expectancy
I wait for you with hurting heart
As I rise at dawn to begin the day anew
In quiet anticipation of your coming

Defenses

I sandbagged the dikes of my heart all day
Keeping busy with meals and dishes
With shopping and cleaning
Now I am ready to close my eyes in sleep
The loneliness and loss of you
Inundate me
Flooding my world
With the pain of missing you

Come Back!

You left me not even an image
To comfort and company me
When you left
I am bereft of your face, your words, you
In quiet emptiness
Pained
I await your certain return

I Wait

Bare black, nerve-shaped trees
Silhouetted sharply against the
western sky
at sunset
Lift their naked arms heavenward
In silent anguish for your coming

A Thousand Nights in One

When the difficulties of life threaten to engulf me
I cry out in anguish
And hear no answering response
I shout in near despair
And my voice reverberates mockingly
I pound the wall in desperation
Nothing, but the hollow echo of emptiness

Why have you left me alone
Bereft of supporting hand and tender voice
Minus even your wordless presence
Why?
When you know you are everything to me
Sun, moon, stars--my reason for existence

There is no light in my life now
Only terrible empty blackness
A thousand nights in one
I could bear the darkness
If I could feel
You here beside me

But there is only the feeling of non feeling
And I wander in this wasteland
In search of you
My beloved

Memo

Can you feel my pain
Across the miles
Over the months
It throbs
A wound tender to the touch
It aches
A steady unremitting emptiness
Waiting to be healed

Out of Control

Shriveled victim of wafting wind
Floating aimlessly, directionless
Passive
Bereft of will to will
Tailspinning
Through the unsympathetic atmosphere
Heading into
Abysmal nothingness

I Seek You

Plato speaks of shadows and images
At least there is something to grasp
However elusive
But you are not even a shadow
And images have no meaning

How can you convince me of the reality beyond
When even the shadows
Which hint at that beyond
Nonexist

In this labyrinthine darkness
Hurting
Hoping, I seek you

Beyond Feeling

There is not even the feeling of non feeling
Just a numbness that defies description
Like fingers iced in the bitter winter air
Seared by the scalding water
In the bathroom sink
No pain, no sensation whatever
Hot and cold becoming one
Neither clearly felt
A new sensation
Created by the oneness of the two

Is there a feeling beyond feeling
Deeper, richer, fuller
Invested with the pain of unfeeling
Of deprivation
Of wild unnamed loneliness
Yet filled with the adventure
Of an uncharted course
The awfulness of unknowing
The truth of discovery

My love for you reached that plateau last night
With you at my side
And I set out into the mazed wilderness
Unfelt
With such intensity
That my heart nearly split into atoms
Exploding in time capsules
As we walked side by side
Through the untamed wilderness

Kingdom Within

I stand at the brink of fathomless blackness
    A lone traveler into the unknown abyss below
    And I fear
    With cold trembling

Only your love could lure me to explore this blasted
    wasteland
    Where darkness is light
    And light but faded remembrance

Triumph

Some speak of pain exquisite
Grief unbearable,
Anguish acute
Intolerable
In each, there is the
Experience of feeling

What of the pain that
Combines, surpasses all of these
Yet calls forth no feeling
So refined and subtle
So elusive and searing

It defies description,
Rejects mitigation
Faith endures
Love alone transcends

Bewildered, Expectant, I Certain Seek

One foot moves dumbly in front
of the other
I scarcely know if I am walking or standing still
And my destination seems now forward
Again backward
I am in some surrealistic nightmare world
Where time stands still
And all movement ceases
To make way for non-movement

The sidewalk rises, a skyscraper barrier
Still I go on
Hoping to find him behind the empty forms
Beneath the distorted images

He will not leave me
To travel this disturbing way alone
I walk on trudgingly
Hopelessly heavy hearted
All the while serene
In the silent surety of his love

Presence

I can hardly look at your home suspended
Firmly from the brownbrick wall bathed
In spotlight
That distorts all else in grotesque shadow
I do not have the key to your house
And you never come out unbidden

Sometimes I fear you have left another way
So empty is my heart
As I gaze at your beloved house
Whose simple contours in the past
Comforted me
When I but glanced at them

Why does it seem
That you have gone far away never to return
When my heart feels the contrary to be so
How can I believe when belief has fled
I know not where

Where shall I turn
In my empty aloneness
But to you
Unseen
Unfelt

Adoration

You are not pure negation
Absence unfelt
Darkness unlit

You are Love
Unfelt
Unseen
And I love you adoringly

Chapter 2

Love and Commitment

As shades do recommend the light.
-Shakespeare

Begins with the same image,
But the opposite passion of the
searching group,
And progresses from moments
of love recalled
To an appreciation
of the eternal;
And from the intensely
emotional
To the serenely intellectual

Beloved

Sentinel trees surrounding my heart
Speak eloquently of you

Intensity

The pain of love crashes over me
Like vast thundering waves
Smashing against the ragged rocks

Your Love Showered Me

The rain came down in soft torrents
Flushing free pain's clinging cobwebs
Cleansing fast life's bitter memories
It slackened
Caressing dearly my wounded heart
Offering balm to soothe my troubled spirit
Your love showered me today

"Bolero"

You fluted to me, Piper,
And I followed your reedy call
All unknowing
Lured by its gentle insistence
Into the forest of darkness and mystery
Accompanied all the while
By the steady rhythmic certainty
Of you unseen by my side

Circle of Concern

We three joined hands across the room
A chintz couch and a Morris chair
separating
Forming a circle of concern
So tight my throat a tourniquet
My pulse a race car
My heart a tympani
To be adjusted for every nuance
By loving hands briefly released
Quickly reclasped
I felt greatly loved

Loneliness Warmed

Snowflake my cold heart
Tonight lonely
With glorious geometric crystals
Scattered scintillating
Their warm whiteness
Clear brilliance
Evidence certain
Of your soundless, silent
Delicate presence
In my adoring heart

Sidewalks of My Heart

In his eyes
I glimpsed the grief of countless griefs
In his voice
I heard the pain of many pains
His words fell like hot teardrops
Burning the sidewalks of my heart
And the supposedly solid concrete
Crumbled willingly
Unable to withstand
The blistering salty flow
The seared edges a mute testimony
To the power of those words
And the bubbling liquid
Filling the tiny cracks
And broad crevices
Evidence of the complete surrender
Of the sidewalk to the elements
Of the heart to the heart

Trust

Your words wrap me round
Until cocooned in their secure
warmth
I am strengthened to endure
The womblike darkness of my
silken shroud
Knowing that but a moment will
pass
And I will emerge to butterfly
the spring
With sudden beauty

Mystery

How is it possible so to love you
With such intensity
I seldom see you
Never touch you

Your voice is unheard melody
Crescendo-ing into a symphony
Your face a rare portrait
Galleried in my inmost being
I long to lay my weary head
Upon your burning heart
To feel your gentle hand
Upon my head in benediction

I am your lamb
Feed me
Your lost sheep
Find me

Response

Your love spiraled softly down
Devastating my high walled barriers
Penetrating my hard shelled defenses
Melting my silent resistance

I surrendered to its snowflake action
Peopling my heart
With myriad forms
Of translucent beauty

Fragrance of You

Inward swung the door
I breathed immediately the scent
of you
Easter lilies trumpeting your
presence
Spicing the air with their
powerful
Heady fragrance
Touching tenderly my inmost
heart
Spreading
Pervading my inmost being

Behind me the diamond-paned
door
Closed decisively
I breathed fresh spring air
And the fragrance of you

Fidelity

I have not left harbor
For lo these many years
Though outfitted and equipped
To venture on long voyages
In uncharted waters
Sturdy and stalwart ship that I am

The anchor of your love
Keeps me moored here

Commitment

Tabernacle me beside you
In the golden mansion
On your silent street
So little visited

I will company you

Journey of Life

You began to die the day you were born
O Infant Godman
Lying helpless Babe in roughstrawed
      manger
You set forth on your salvation journey
Each moment lovegift recorded
In the Father's eternal redemption book

Seraphic Stephen radianced your grace
Guiltless Innocents, too, helpless holy
John, beloved Mary's caretaker
Gospeled in love
Family holy, Joseph, Mary and You
Cocooned
Kings offered anointing
Myrrh and allegiance
Followers honored, honoring,
Spoke with their lives
To those with ears to hear
Hearts to listen
Of joyous, fleeting Christmas
Lent, necessary crossinterim
Easter, forever alleluia

Omnipotence Accommodated

Pathless skies stretch in endless magnitude
Oceans in their violence and calm
Await Your word
Fire, snow, heat, cold You permit
And control
Endless diversity, artistic
Inspiring, awesome

Omnipotent God,
You who created the universe
    Vast
    Measureless
    Incomprehensible
Consented to be pinioned to a rude cross
    To die
    To spend three days in tombed
    oblivion
    To await Resurrection victory

You who formed great mastodons
        Gave tigers stripes
        Adders poison
Permitted a crude cow to low you to sleep
A simple, clumsy donkey to warm you
With his breath

You who called forth mighty crashing waves
        Fierce winds
        Great glaciers
Peopled the deep with immense whales
        Oysters housing translucent
        Beauty
        Brilliant-hued fish
        In shape and variety uncounted
You who fashioned flowers uncounted, diverse
        Trees and vines in artistic form
        Harvests rich and billowing
Contented yourself to use them as

Illustrations
      Lilies of the field
      in Solomon glory
      Good fruit from good tree
      Abundant harvest,
      Fruitful vineyard

You who made the unseen come alive
Become believable
Pearl of great price
Jonah
Who used night to rest and pray
Day to teach and heal
You became subject to your subjects
      Receiver of your word
      Guide to the wanderer
      Home to the homeless
      All things to all people

Jesus, God Man,
      Continually You bend down
      To us, Your errant children,
      In our trembling inadequacy
      Accommodating yourself to us

Chapter Three

Nature

All I have seen
Teaches me to trust the Creator
For all I have not seen.

-Ralph Waldo Emerson

It is from the voice of created things,
that we discover the voice of God
never ceasing to woo our lives.

-Maurice Gaudefroy

A seasonal progression, with three
winter views of the moon,
beginning with death and ending
with affirmation.

Mourning

Thrust back on its scaly
black body
Suspended sinuously
In the barely outlined
blackness
of predawn October
The great brown shredded
adder
Mouth open in anguish
unspeakable
A Guernica figure
death ugly and graphic
Shrieks its pain
At the tragic loss of its bairn
branch
Lying torn, bleeding
on the silent dew wet grass
Helpless victim of wind
whip and storm lash

My father died this morning

Autumn Carnage

Limbs all akimbo
Sprawl bloodless dismembered
Spotting the fall green carpet
Blood red
Sickly yellow

Splayed prodigally
In vast reckless disarray
Spattering the leaf-mottled lawn
Helpless
In death throes severed
They await removal

Rough clad rescuers hoist them
Unceremoniously into the
Battered red pickup,
Piling high their
Crushed and matted frames
To make elimination swift and
Efficient

Grieving trees sough mournfully

A Distorted Loveliness

Midnight predawn reveals
spotlighted obliquely
Crumpled fallweary leaves
freefalling
Landing randomly directionless
on sodden unyielding pitch
Emerging transformed

Bizarre geometric figures
Curiously artistic

Direction

A shoe
Of driftwood
Twirled its way
Shoreward

Then
Pointed its watery toe
Toward
Infinity

Goodbye

Waft, leaves, bid farewell
Float gently to join crisp piles
Adieu, fading fall

Youth's Frolic

Beneath firm, fun steps
Leaves crunch fitfully
Child's play, adult's lark

Stark Grandeur

Bare, black trees emerge
Between gold, russet, orange leaves
Winter's bleak preface

Paradox

Rich-hued trees denuded
Seem stark, barren, sterile now
Life pulsates within

Oriental Montage

Yellow ginko fans
Dot the leaf-sprinkled meadow
Pretend pagoda

Sunlight on the Hudson

In glancing water
A thousand glinting lights
Starry, starry night

Haiku
Scintillate, sparkle
O grave, now-ruffled Hudson
Morning water show

Autumn Meditation

Against the winter blue sky
Stripped branches
Nerves exposed
Spire skyward
Green expanse a startling
contrast

Dead they seem
Those November-leafless trees
Oak, beach, elm
Evergreens by contrast
Lush and richly full
Their sweeping brush
branches
Silent proclaimers of life

I walk the still winding road
Empty tree lined
Poignantly aware
Of those desolate trees
Throbbing with life
Less than nine months away
Speculating
On a winter landscape
Devoid of trees

I am reminded
Of prairie settlers
Rolvaag's *Giants in the Earth*
And their vast treeless terrain
Awesome and frightening
In scope endless

Faced with eliminating
Grotesque unlovely shapes
Exposed in raw ugliness
At winter's onset
I walk the silent winding road
Bare tree lined
Vibrantly aware
Of each separate species
Pondering

To be deprived
Of less-than-nine-months-away
Freshness
Spring life
Of the panoramic profusion
Of fall

Georgia O'Keefe grandeur
Great stark shapes
And delicately artistic
Still life branches
A void not to be considered

You are emptiness
Waiting to be filled
O multi-armed trunk
You are a fruitful womb,
O sterile seeming tree
I choose you
And life

Time Unnoticed

Drybrown, crispyellow
They crackle invitingly
Under scuffling feet
November, slipping
gradually
Into December's austere
whiteness

Challenge

Brownwet spears
Cut through
The swiftflowing river
Sure and true
Plunging intrepidly
Into the heart
Of their sometime waterfoe

"Lunar Acceptance"

If I would paint you, O slightly
Shivered from full Moon,
And the wedge-shaped patches of lunar light
You send to illumine for a frozen moment
Select sections of silent passive earth
One road leading to the convent cemetery
The other to the outside world

At their apex,
Framed in the midnight-black field,
The stone Agony diptych
Blue white, evergreen foiled
Its ministering angel proffering
A moonfull chalice
To the kneeling Jesus
Triangled in light
Immobile in pain and willed
acceptance

40

Epiphany

You reveal yourself startlingly
sparing
Through winter's shivered
branches
Cold brilliant light
Swathing delicate paths

You charge the night with moon
magic

Shadows of the Image

I would like to capture on canvas
Moon relieved blackness
In all its magic
Vividly
Truthfully

Shadows of the wondrous image,
Words,
Must suffice

Request

Reach down,
Gentle Ursa,
And scoop me up
Into the calm, clear blackness
Of your heavenly home

Victim

Ripped from its socket untimely
The brown blood limb lies diagonal
Against the massive elephantine trunk
Of ageless copper beach
Redtipped arms outspread
Weeping bloody tears
Mourning the loss of its bairn branch
So lately victim
Of wind whip
Storm harsh
Spring violence

Winter Sunrise

The sun rose softly
Behind the dark brownwinter
trees suffusing the January
sky
With a crescent of delicate
rose

Winter Scene

In the December sub zero
Snow
Feather frosted the
Evergreens
Icing their branches
With marshmallow waves
Delicate meringue
Slightly tip curled
Shivering weightless
Beneath the chill arctic sun

Snow Experience

The gentle snow
Sprinkled my glasses softly
Tingled my cheek tenderly
Touched delicately my
chapped lips

I tasted beauty
Felt the ephemeral
Experienced nature
Praised God

In The Wake Of The Jet

Swifter than the speed of sound
The vanishing jet cut a volcanic swath
In the February morning sky
leaving in its wake
A glorious heavenly ribbon
To festoon the winter firmament
lingeringly

Mesmerized
I gazed at the slowly widening
ribbon radiance
Arch of subtle reds and pinks
Edged with delicate cloudlace
Gradually burgeoning into puffcloud
borders
To decorate the unresistant skyblue
background
With a fragmentary Etna of morning
brilliance

Promise of Spring

Invite me to stoop low
And examine
The poignant remnant of
fragile winter beauty
Bowing humbly graceful
before the dawn
A cluster of snowbells
Nestled amid brown bare
surroundings

Early Arrival

He came early
February 8, to be exact,
A chill still-winter day
To pursue his suit

High in the slender naked
magnolia tree
He sought his unseen beloved
Insistently
Repeatedly
His persistent song piercing
The early morning air
And my heart
With his longing

I think she had not yet arrived
The cardinal flew off
Elsewhere to seek her

Death Wish

When I am dying
Carry me out to the snow
blanketed meadow
Stretching virgin vast

Lay me down in the eider soft
snow
Facing the circle of great iced
pines
And sylvan snow piled, bare
branched trees

Let me contemplate
this winter white fairyland,
Earth,
Before I close my eyes to life

Resurrection

Dense fog shrouded tomb
Hesitant sun rolls back veil
Nuns alleluia

Harbingers of Spring

Forerunners humble
Shy teardrops, tiny, demure
Snowbells welcome spring

Healing Wind

O gentle to vehement March
wind
Blow the cobwebs from her
shrouded mind
Free Lenore from withering depression
Cleanse her from dread
cancer
Abolish necessary
chemotherapy

Let her feel your healing
breath
Offer her serene promise of
new life
Lift up her heart with the
wonder of Spring
Refresh tenderly her
sometimes flagging spirit
Renew her with uplifting,
unremitting joy

Farewell

Poised above the Spanish
tiled roof
Absorbed gradually into
melting morning
Fragile wisp of moon

Compassion

Weep, O Willow,
For the pained and suffering
of the world
Umbrella them beneath the
sure canopy
Of your comforting presence

Anticipation

Rhododendron on the hill are
peeking pink
These mid-May days
Sunshine and warm weather
Will summarily radiance the
hillside
With ardent fuchsia and
delicate lavender

Invocation

Bleached branches lift barren
arms heavenward
Pleading for fresh spring
garments
To clothe their nakedness in
raiment
Like the lilies of surpassing
splendor
Who neither sow nor reap
Yet outshine Solomon in all
his glory

Dogwood

Forging through the fragrant
woods
Bird serenaded
I came abruptly upon an
unexpected arc of dead
And grieved it should be so

Until I gazed upward

Spider

Did a wayward bird
Or a careless bat
Mistake your gossamer home
For a wind tunnel?
He made a gaping hole in it.

Where did you go?

And God Looked...

Naked
They reveal pristine beauty
Only winter sees them unclothed
Branches artistically arranged
Creating lovely fluid lines
Sharply defined geometric shapes
Stark black and white photographic
effect
Framing sun, moon, light

Fresh green in spring sprightly
Comfortable shady attire for
searing summer
Offering certain shelter,
creative camouflage
Full, June-lush trees, green
deepening landscape
Stage for autumn's panoramic
advent
Multitudinous colors
Splashed in fall abundance
An artist's palette used prodigally
Preparing for winter's stripping

And God looked on all he had created
And it was very good

About the Author

SISTER PAULA MARIE is a member of the Sisters of Christian Charity. She lives in Camp Hill, Pennsylvania where she is engaged in Pastoral Care ministry at Holy Spirit Hospital. She was a high school English teacher for many years and presently teaches creative writing to a class of eighth graders and to a group of adult women. She has a B.S. in Education and an M.A. in English from Seton Hall University. She is also a certified library media specialist. This is her first book of poetry.